WHSmith

Practise
Percentages
KS3
Age 11–14
Hilary Koll and Steve Mills

Contents

Introduction

Practise Percentages

Practise Percentages is for anyone who is struggling to understand concepts in percentages like calculating percentages of quantities and doing percentage increases and decreases, as well as all the other difficult ideas usually covered in maths lessons at Key Stage 3. Percentages is a topic that most people find difficult at first, but this simple, step-by-step approach should have you calculating percentages in your head and on a calculator in no time.

Part 1 (pages 3–14) of this book is all about understanding percentages, estimating and calculating them and converting them to fractions and decimals. Part 2 (pages 19–30) deals with percentage change, including finding percentage increases and decreases in real-life problems. Also covered is writing an amount as a percentage of another amount.

How to use *Practise*

Work through each section in order, reading all the clues and tips in the margins as you go through the exercises. You will need to cut out the cards in the centre of the book to use for some activities. Make sure you keep these cards in a safe place, such as an envelope, so you can re-use them.

When you feel confident with what is written on a particular page, turn over and try to answer the questions on the next page. Carefully mark all your answers and see how you got on. If you are still stuck and feel that you need some more practice, try some of the activities again or re-read the tips and comments in the margins. If you feel confident and have got most of the questions right, move on to the next section.

You might find it helpful to make a list of all the key words you come across in this book and write down the meanings. This will help you when you try to answer the questions.

First published in 2007
exclusively for WHSmith by
Hodder Education, an Hachette UK company
338 Euston Road
London NW1 3BH

Impression number   10 9 8 7 6 5 4 3
Year   2011
Text and illustrations © Hodder Murray 2007

Text: Hilary Koll and Steve Mills (e-mail: info@cmeprojects.com)
Cover illustration by Sally Newton Illustrations
Typeset by Fakenham Photosetting Limited, Fakenham, Norfolk
Printed and bound in Spain

A CIP record for this book is available from the British Library

ISBN 978 0 340 94290 1

Estimating percentages

Practice

Percentages tell us how much of a whole something is.

- Cut out all the percentage cards on page 15.

100% This card is **one hundred per cent** and it means 'the whole'.

(100% of them were male.) (The shirt is 100% cotton.) (I scored 100% in a test.)

75% This card is **seventy-five per cent** and it means 'three-quarters'.

(75% of them were male.) (The shirt is 75% cotton.) (I scored 75% in a test.)

50% This card is **fifty per cent** and it means 'a half'.

(50% of them were male.) (The shirt is 50% cotton.) (I scored 50% in a test.)

25% This card is **twenty-five per cent** and it means 'a quarter'.

(25% of them were male.) (The shirt is 25% cotton.) (I scored 25% in a test.)

0% This card is **zero per cent** and it means 'none' or 'nothing'.

(0% of them were male.) (The shirt is 0% cotton.) (I scored 0% in a test.)

Estimating

Making an estimate is like having a good guess at something. It happens all the time in real life.

Imagine that a footballer has hurt his ankle. His manager might make an estimate as to how likely he is to play on Saturday. He might say, 'There's a 60% chance that he'll be better by then.'

Don't worry about estimating

People sometimes worry that their estimates will be wrong. It does not matter if the manager was not exactly right – it was just an estimate to give people some idea.

Do not worry, just practise saying roughly what percentage of each container in **Try it yourself!** is filled.

Try it yourself!

Estimate what percentage of each container is filled and find a card showing that percentage.

  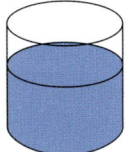 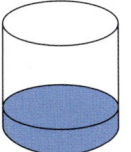  

Clues and tips

When estimating, always keep percentages such as 75%, 50% and 25% in mind.

Think to yourself:

> Is it more or less than a half, a quarter or three-quarters?

What next?

If you are fine with estimating percentages, go on to page 5. If not, cut out two different-coloured circles from card. On each circle make a straight cut to the centre. Slide them together like this:

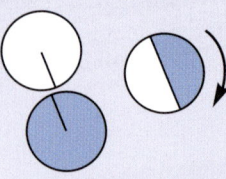

Twist them to create different percentages of a circle (as in question 2).

Now practise estimating what percentage of the circle is shaded.

Try it yourself!

1. By drawing lines, match each container with an appropriate **estimate**.

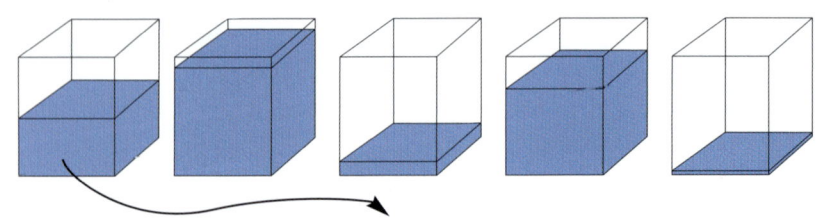

About 0% full	About 5% full	About 10% full	About 20% full	About 50% full	About 65% full	About 75% full	About 95% full	About 100% full

2. By drawing lines, match each shape with an appropriate **estimate**.

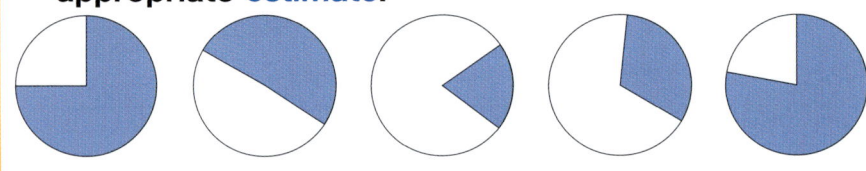

About 0% shaded	About 10% shaded	About 20% shaded	About 35% shaded	About 50% shaded	About 65% shaded	About 75% shaded	About 80% shaded	About 100% shaded

3. **Estimate** roughly what percentage of each shape is shaded.

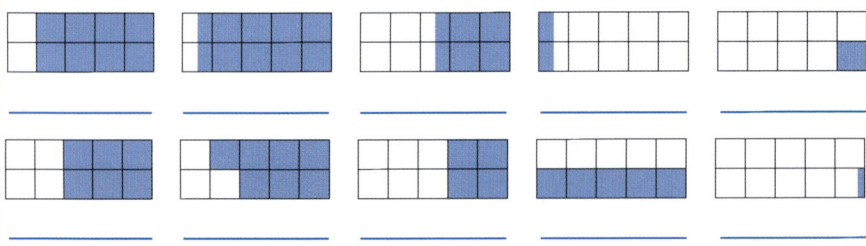

Out of 100

Practice

- Instead of having to guess a percentage, it helps if the shape or container shows 100 equal parts.

  $\boxed{53\%}$ is 53 out of 100 equal parts

  Each percentage can be written in three different ways. As a:

  (percentage)   (fraction)   (division)

  53%   or $\dfrac{53}{100}$ or $53 \div 100$

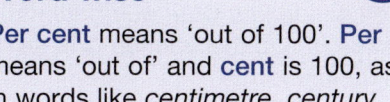

- Some percentages can be written as **fractions** in *more than one* way. Write each of these as a fraction (out of 100).

  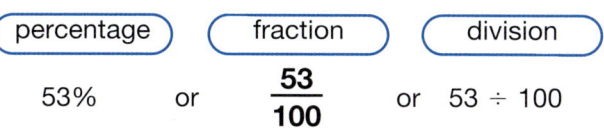

  $\boxed{50\%}$ $\boxed{10\%}$ $\boxed{25\%}$ $\boxed{75\%}$ $\boxed{20\%}$

  $\dfrac{50}{100}$ ——   ——   ——   ——

- Notice that each fraction can be changed to its **simplest form** by dividing the top and bottom numbers by the same number. Change each fraction above to its simplest form by dividing.

  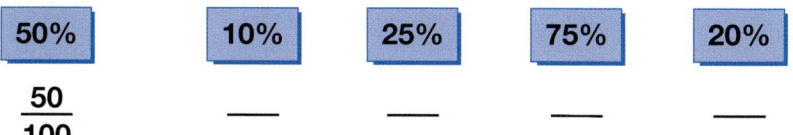

  $\div 50$ $\div 10$ $\div 25$ $\div 25$ $\div 20$

  $\dfrac{50}{100}$ $\dfrac{1}{2}$

  $\div 50$ $\div 10$ $\div 25$ $\div 25$ $\div 20$

- So, 50% can be written as $\dfrac{50}{100}$ or $\dfrac{1}{2}$.

Try it yourself!

Pick a percentage card and describe it:

- as a **fraction** (out of 100)
- and as a **division question** (divided by 100).

Do this several times to get the hang of it.

Always think of the % sign as 'out of 100' or 'divided by 100'.

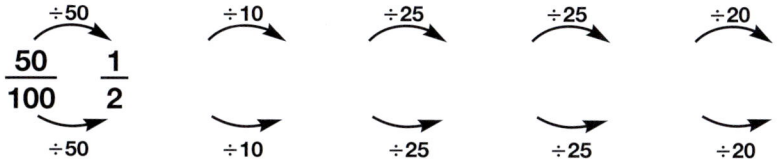

Why percentages?

Percentages are used in everyday life in all sorts of different ways. Look out for these ways, such as:

- Sale 50% off
- Bloggs Bank offers 5% interest on savings
- Smith: only 60% chance of playing in match

Word wise

Per cent means 'out of 100'. **Per** means 'out of' and **cent** is 100, as in words like *centimetre*, *century*.

Simplest form

A **fraction** can be changed to its **simplest form** by dividing the top number (the numerator) and bottom number (the denominator) by the same number.

Clues and tips

When changing a fraction to its simplest form, always look to see what number will divide exactly into the top number (the numerator) and the bottom number (the denominator).

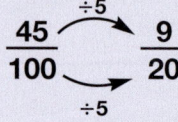

$$\frac{45}{100} \xrightarrow{\div 5} \frac{9}{20}$$
$$\div 5$$

After dividing, check that there is not another whole number that will divide into both numbers. If there is not, the fraction is in its simplest form.

What next?

If you are fine with this topic, go on to page 7.

If not, read the tips above about how to change a fraction to its simplest form.

(You might also find the *Practise Fractions and decimals* book in this series useful.)

Try it yourself!

1. Approximately what percentage of each container is filled?

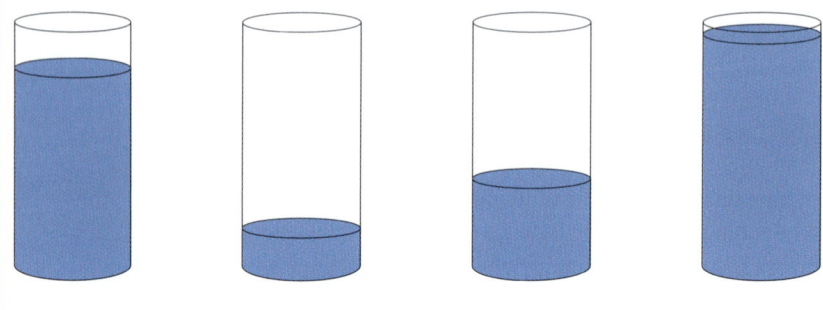

_____   _____   _____   _____

2. Write these percentages as fractions out of 100.

13% $\frac{13}{100}$ 27%   81%   99%

39%   11%   2%   47%

3. Write these percentages as division questions.

55% $55 \div 100$ 38% _____   84% _____

13% _____   6% _____   10% _____

4. Write these percentages as fractions out of 100. Then change each fraction to its simplest form.

20% $\frac{20}{100} \xrightarrow{\div 20} \frac{1}{5}$ 10%   75%
$$\div 20$$

5%   80%   2%

Percentages, fractions and decimals

Practice

- Percentages, fractions and decimals are like three different languages. They are just different ways of describing the same thing.

- Remember that percentages can be written as **fractions** and that some percentages can be written as *more than one* fraction, for example:

  50% can be written as $\dfrac{50}{100}$ or $\dfrac{1}{2}$

- Percentages can also be written as **decimals**. It is easy if the percentage is written as a **division question**.
  24% is 24 ÷ 100
  $24 \div 100 = 0.24$

  > Work this division question out in your head or using a calculator to get a decimal answer.

Try it yourself!

Pick a percentage card and write it as a **division question**.

Then work out the answer as a **decimal** in your head or using a calculator.

42% $42 \div 100 = 0.42$

Look for a pattern as to what happens when you divide a number by 100. You will soon discover how easy it is.

Remember these rules:

Percentage

Write the number out of 100   **32%**   Divide the number by 100

Fraction

$\dfrac{32}{100}$

If possible, change the fraction to its simplest form.

$\div 4$
$\dfrac{32}{100}$ → $\dfrac{8}{25}$
$\div 4$

Decimal

$32 \div 100 = 0.32$

> This has shown that:
> $32\% = \dfrac{8}{25} = 0.32$

Percentages, fractions and decimals

Percentages, fractions and decimals are all used to describe what part of a whole something is.

If someone asked what proportion of a class was girls, the answer could be given as a fraction, e.g. $\dfrac{1}{2}$, as a percentage, e.g. 50%, or as a decimal, e.g. 0.5.

Dividing by 100

It is easy to divide by 100 in your head.

Just move the digits of the number two places to the right. The decimal point remains in the same place.

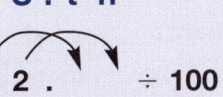

H T U . t h

4 2 . ÷ 100
0 . 4 2

Notice that we write 0.42 rather than .42 as it is easy to miss the decimal point otherwise.

Try it yourself!

1. **Divide each of these numbers by 100 in your head.**

25 __0.25__   32 _____   67 _____   21 _____   86 _____

5 _____   3 _____   20 _____   50 _____   80 _____

2. **Convert each percentage into a decimal in your head.**

55% __55 ÷ 100 = 0.55__   35% _____   74% _____

18% _____   7% _____   32% _____

10% _____   99% _____   100% _____

1% _____   40% _____   33% _____

3. **Convert each percentage into a fraction and decimal.**

Percentage	Fraction (in its simplest form)	Decimal
30%	$\frac{30}{100} = \frac{3}{10}$	0.3
90%		
2%		
15%		
8%		

Calculating percentages in your head

- There are many different ways to **calculate** a percentage of a number in your head.

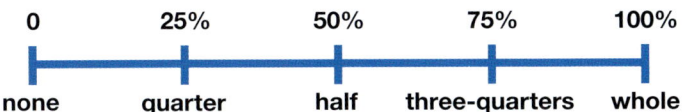

0	25%	50%	75%	100%
none	quarter	half	three-quarters	whole

Remember first that 50% is $\frac{1}{2}$, 25% is $\frac{1}{4}$ and 75% is $\frac{3}{4}$.
Here are some of the ways:

- To calculate **50%**:   halve the number.
  50% of £300 → **half** of £300   = £150
  50% of 820 g → **half** of 820 g   = 410 g

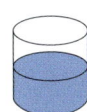

- To calculate **25%**:   halve the number and halve the answer
  (or just divide by 4).
  25% of £300 → **half** of £300 = £150 → **half** of £150 = £75
  25% of 820 g → **half** of 820 g = 410 g → **half** of 410 g = 205 g

- To calculate **75%**:   halve the number and halve the answer.
  Then add the two answers together.
  75% of £300 → **half** of £300 = £150 → **half** of £150 = £75
  → £150 + £75 = £225
  75% of 820 g → **half** of 820 g = 410 g → **half** of 410 g = 205 g
  → 410 g + 205 g = 615 g

Try it yourself!

You will need these three percentage cards from page 15. Also cut out the number cards on page 17.

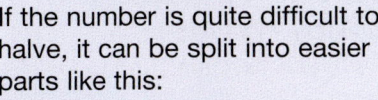
| 50% | 25% | 75% |

Pick a number card and a percentage card and **calculate** that percentage of the number in your head.

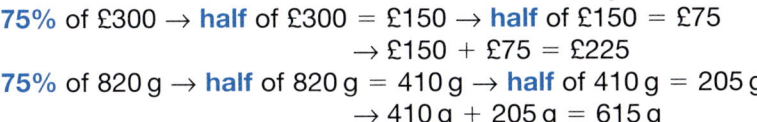
| 50% | of | 120 | = 60 |

Do this as many times as you can until you get the hang of it.

Word wise

Calculate does *not* mean 'use a calculator'.
It means 'work out the answer'.
You can calculate in your head, on paper or using a calculator.

Halving numbers

If the number is quite difficult to halve, it can be split into easier parts like this:

Half of 172

Split 172 into parts . . .

| 100 | 70 | 2 |

and halve each part.

| 50 | 35 | 1 |

Then add them back together again.

Half of 172 =
50 + 35 + 1 = 86

The number can be split in different ways:

Half of 172

Split 172 into parts . . .

| 160 | 12 |

and halve each part.

| 80 | 6 |

So

Half of 172 = 80 + 6 = 86

Clues and tips

If the number is quite difficult to halve, it can be split into easier parts.

Use a number line

If you find it difficult to keep track of numbers in your head, you might find this useful.

Draw a line like this:

```
0     25%  50%  75% 100%
├──────┼────┼────┼────┤
```

Write the amount underneath the 100%, like this:

```
0     25%  50%  75% 100%
├──────┼────┼────┼────┤
                    680
```

Then, as you work out 50% and 25%, etc., write them under the line.

```
0     25%  50%  75% 100%
├──────┼────┼────┼────┤
      170  340  510  680
```

What next?

If you are fine with this topic, go on to page 11. If not, read the tips above again and practise more with the cut-out cards.

Try it yourself!

1. Calculate each of these percentages in your head.

50% of £600 <u>£300</u>	50% of £120 _____	50% of £680 _____
50% of 72 kg _____	50% of 48 kg _____	50% of 840 kg _____
25% of £600 _____	25% of £120 _____	25% of £680 _____
25% of 72 kg _____	25% of 48 kg _____	25% of 840 kg _____
75% of £600 _____	75% of £120 _____	75% of £680 _____
75% of 72 kg _____	75% of 48 kg _____	75% of 840 kg _____

2. Calculate each of these percentages in your head.

25% of £160 _____	50% of £110 _____	75% of £88 _____
50% of 70 kg _____	25% of 180 kg _____	50% of 290 kg _____
75% of 16 ml _____	75% of 140 ml _____	25% of 460 ml _____
25% of 144 m _____	75% of 36 m _____	50% of 184 m _____

3. Calculate each of the percentages to solve these problems.

In a sale you pay 75% of the ticket price.
The ticket price for a coat is £56.
How much is the sale price? _____

A man pays 25% of his earnings in tax.
He earns £24 000 in a year.
How much tax does he pay? _____

A mobile phone company has a 50% sale.
How much will a phone cost in the sale
if it usually costs £78? _____

Calculating other percentages

Practice

- Other percentages can be found in your head by first finding 10%.

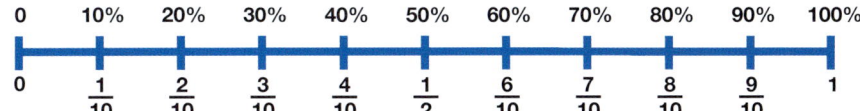

0	10%	20%	30%	40%	50%	60%	70%	80%	90%	100%

| 0 | $\frac{1}{10}$ | $\frac{2}{10}$ | $\frac{3}{10}$ | $\frac{4}{10}$ | $\frac{1}{2}$ | $\frac{6}{10}$ | $\frac{7}{10}$ | $\frac{8}{10}$ | $\frac{9}{10}$ | 1 |

- To calculate **10%**: divide the number by 10.
  10% of £300 → £300 ÷ **10** = £30
  10% of 820 g → 820 g ÷ **10** = 82 g

- To calculate **20%**: divide by 10 and double.
  20% of £300 → £300 ÷ **10** = £30 → £30 × **2** = £60
  20% of 820 g → 820 g ÷ **10** = 82 g → 82 g × **2** = 164 g

- To calculate **30%**: divide by 10 and multiply by 3.
  30% of £300 → £300 ÷ **10** = £30 → £30 × **3** = £90
  30% of 820 g → 820 g ÷ **10** = 82 g → 82 g × **3** = 246 g

- To calculate **40%**: divide by 10 and multiply by 4.

> For *all percentages that are multiples of 10*, the answer to 10% can be used to **calculate** percentages of amounts.

Try it yourself!

You will need the percentage cards that show multiples of 10 and the number cards from page 17.

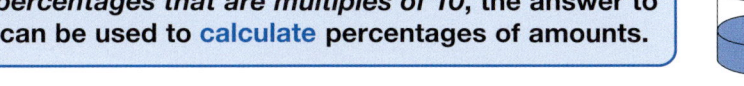

| 10% | 20% | 30% | 40% | 50% | 60% | 70% | 80% | 90% |

Pick a number card and a percentage card and **calculate** that percentage of the number in your head.

30% of **120** = 12 × 3 = 36

Do this as many times as you can until you get the hang of it.

Check that the answer is 'about right'.

30% is just a bit more than 25% or $\frac{1}{4}$.

$\frac{1}{4}$ of 120 = 30.   **36 is a bit more than 30.**

So it is about right.

Dividing by 10

Remember that when a number is **divided** by 10, the digits move one place to the **right**.

```
H T U . t h
1 4 0 .        ÷ 10
  1 4 . 0
```

There is no need to write a zero at the right-hand end of a decimal.

14.0 = 14
50.0 = 50

A different way for 90%

When finding 90%, first find 10%. Rather than multiplying the answer by 9, sometimes it might be easier to subtract 10% from the original answer (100%), like this:

> **Find 90% of 120.**

10% of 120 = 12

Then, rather than calculating 12 × **9** to find **90%**, subtract 12 from 120.

120 − 12 = 108
so **90% of 120 = 108**

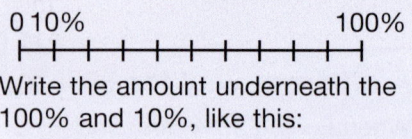
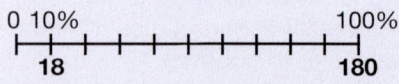
Try it yourself!

1. Calculate each of these percentages in your head.

10% of £600	**£60**	10% of £120 _____	10% of £680 _____
10% of 72 kg	**7.2 kg**	10% of 48 kg _____	10% of 84 kg _____
20% of £600 _____		20% of £120 _____	20% of £680 _____
20% of 72 kg _____		20% of 48 kg _____	20% of 84 kg _____

2. Calculate each of these percentages in your head.

30% of £60 _____	60% of £40 _____	80% of £90 _____
40% of 70 kg _____	90% of 110 kg _____	20% of 35 kg _____
70% of 80 ml _____	40% of 120 ml _____	80% of 300 ml _____
90% of 140 m _____	70% of 110 km _____	30% of 184 m _____

3. Calculate each of the percentages to solve these problems.

In a sale you pay 80% of the ticket price.
The ticket price for a coat is £60.
How much is the sale price? _____

A woman pays 30% of her earnings in tax.
She earns £12 000 in a year.
How much tax does she pay? _____

A baby girl weighs 90% of her expected weight.
Her expected weight was 130 ounces.
How much does she weigh? _____

Calculating percentages with a calculator

Practice

- Because a percentage can be written as a fraction or decimal, there are different ways of calculating percentages on a **calculator**.

As a fraction

Remember that a percentage can be written as a fraction 'out of 100' or 'divided by 100'.

To find **32% of £146** on a calculator, 32% can be keyed in as a **fraction**.

 $\dfrac{32}{100} \times £146 = £46.72$ ⟵ Key into the calculator 32 ÷ 100 and then × 146

Notice that the **multiplication key** is used in place of the word 'of'.

As a decimal

Another way is to write each percentage as a decimal. Remind yourself how on page 7.

To find **32% of £146** on a calculator, 32% can be keyed in as a **decimal**.

$0.32 \times £146 = £46.72$

Choose which way you like best and remember to use the multiplication key in place of the word 'of'.

- Always remember to check your answer, whichever way you do it.

32% of £146 = £46.72

Remind yourself how on page 7.

> **check**
>
> **32%** is slightly less than one-third.
> $\frac{1}{3}$ of £150 = £50
> £46.72 is slightly less than £50. So it is about right.

A different way of looking at it

There are different ways of solving percentage questions.
Here is another method.

> Find 27% of 172.

First, find what **1%** of this number is.

172 divided by 100

Then multiply to find what **27%** is.

1.72 × 27

It does not matter which way this is done – the answer will be the same.

Check it

Check to get a rough idea of the size the answer should be. Always round the percentage and the number to make a rough calculation to see if the answer is about right.

Try it yourself!

You will need all your percentage cards, the number cards from page 17 and a calculator.

the number cards from page 17

| 10% | 2% | 15% | 3% | 53% | 99% | 18% | 28% |

Pick a number card and a percentage card, and **calculate** that percentage of the number on a calculator.

| 53% | of | 120 | = 63.6

Do this as many times as you can until you get the hang of it.
Do not forget to check your answers.

Try it yourself!

1. Calculate each of these percentages on a calculator.

32% of £60 _____   64% of £48 _____   88% of £97 _____

42% of 70 kg _____   18% of 112 kg _____   46% of 35 kg _____

17% of 87 ml _____   29% of 125 ml _____   82% of 305 ml _____

99% of 145 m _____   72% of 118 m _____   36% of 184 m _____

2. Solve these problems using a calculator.

In a sale you pay 84% of the ticket price.
The ticket price for a coat is £24.
How much is the sale price?   _____

A man pays 28% of his earnings in tax.
He earns £15 000 in a year.
How much tax does he pay?   _____

A baby girl weighs 86% of her expected weight.
If her expected weight was 130 ounces,
how much does she weigh?   _____

A car is travelling at 54 mph. It slows down
to travel at 67% of that speed.
How fast is the car travelling now?   _____

I have £365 in my bank account.
I earn 3.5% interest on this money.
How much interest do I earn?   _____

A restaurant adds a 12% service charge to the
cost of a meal. How much is the service charge
for a meal costing £35?   _____

Activity cards

20%	80%	5%	0%	41%	71%	99%
10%	70%	3%	15%	39%	67%	95%
75%	60%	2%	12%	32%	65%	100%
25%	40%	1%	11%	28%	53%	85%
50%	30%	90%	7%	23%	45%	72%

Activity cards

Activity cards

200	140	180	660	360
80	760	580	420	320
40	800	340	480	280
120	160	260	220	240

Writing something as a percentage

- Up to now, almost every question in this book has had a percentage in it. Like these:

> Convert this percentage into a decimal: **55%**

> Calculate **32%** of £60.

> In a sale you pay **84%** of the ticket price.
> The ticket price for a coat is £24.
> How much is the sale price?

For these types of questions, remember that the **%** sign means 'out of 100' or 'divided by 100'.

- The questions that follow do *not* have a percentage in them. In these questions the ANSWER is a percentage.

Like this:

> Jo got 54 marks in a test out of a total of 60 marks.
> Give Jo's score as a **percentage**.

No percentage given

Answer will be a percentage

- For this type of question:

a) write a number as a **fraction** of another
b) multiply by 100.   **(Yes, it is that easy.)**

a) Jo got 54 out of 60. Write this as a **fraction**.
b) Then multiply by 100.

$$\frac{54}{60} \times 100$$

> Key into the calculator
> 54 ÷ 60 and then × 100

Try this on a calculator. Do you get the answer 90%?
Notice that your ANSWER is a percentage.

Now try this one.

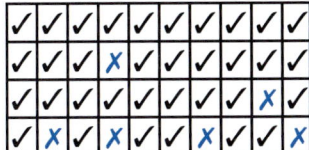

> Rob got 34 marks in a test out of a total of 40 marks.
> Give Rob's score as a percentage.

$$\frac{34}{40} \times 100 = 85\%$$

By changing both scores to percentages they can be compared to find out who scored the highest proportion of marks.

Fraction line

When looking at a fraction, think of the line separating the two numbers as a **division** sign. When keying a fraction into a calculator, key in the top number (the numerator) and the divide sign, then the bottom number (the denominator). Like this:

$$\frac{1}{2} = 1 \div 2$$

$$\frac{3}{4} = 3 \div 4$$

In your head

Without a calculator, change the fraction to its simplest form first (see page 6).

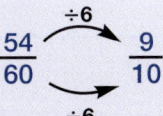

It is easier to multiply this by 100 in your head. Then, if possible, divide the denominator and 100 by the same number.

$$\frac{9}{10} \times 100 \,{}^{\div 10}_{}$$

$$= 9 \times 10 = 90\%$$

Try it yourself!

1. **Give the first number as a percentage of the second number.**
   You can use a calculator. Round any decimals to 2 decimal places.

   60 out of 75 $\frac{60}{75} \times \mathbf{100} = \mathbf{80\%}$ 51 out of 60 _____

   48 out of 52 _____   11 out of 55 _____

   58 out of 80 _____   112 out of 120 _____

   45 out of 70 _____   40 out of 65 _____

2. **Give each of these scores as a percentage. You can use a calculator. Round any decimals to 2 decimal places.**
   Who scored the highest percentage of marks?

   Matt got 42 marks out of a total of 50 marks. _____

   Richard got 64 marks out of a total of 70 marks. _____

   Nicole got 73 marks out of a total of 80 marks. _____

   Michelle got 33 marks out of a total of 40 marks. _____

   Tom got 105 marks out of a total of 120 marks. _____

   Jodie got 81 marks out of a total of 90 marks. _____

3. **Answer these questions *without* using a calculator.**

   There were 150 people at a concert.
   60 of the people were female.
   What percentage were female? _____

   There were 160 people at a funfair.
   96 of the people were female.
   What percentage were female? _____

Problems, problems

Practice

- Most people find percentages difficult because percentage problems and puzzles always look very different from each other.

> **12% of a 150 g chocolate bar is nuts. How many grams of nuts are there?**

> **24 out of every 300 people in the country wear contact lenses. What is this as a percentage?**

> **A bank paid Anna some interest on the £180 she had in the bank. It paid her £32. What is this as a percentage?**

> **A pack of biscuits usually has 20 biscuits. In a new pack, 15% more biscuits are included. How many extra biscuits is that?**

Remember this

Do make sure that you read the question carefully to check you understand what it is asking for. Try to imagine the situation, drawing a small picture to help you, if you like.

When you see a problem, do not panic!
Ask yourself these questions:

> **Has the question got a percentage in it?**

Or   > **Am I supposed to give a percentage as an ANSWER?**

Forgotten how?

If you have forgotten how to answer both types of questions, look at page 13 for the first type and page 19 for the second type.

Divide by 100 if the question contains a percentage.

Multiply by 100 to get a percentage ANSWER.

- If the question has a percentage in it, remember that the percentage sign means 'out of 100' or 'divided by 100'.

> **12% of a 150 g chocolate bar is nuts. How many grams of nuts are there?**

12% of 150 g

 $\dfrac{12}{100} \times 150\ g = 18\ g$

- If the ANSWER is to be a percentage, write the fraction and then multiply by 100.

> **24 out of every 300 people in the country wear contact lenses. What is this as a percentage?**

$\dfrac{24}{300} \times 100 = 8\%$

> **Look carefully at every problem to work out which type it is. (Sometimes there might be an extra part to the question – these are looked at on the next few pages.)**

Try it yourself!

1. **Solve these problems.**

   14% of a 250 g pot of yogurt is strawberries. $\dfrac{14}{100} \times 250\,g = 35\,g$
   How many grams of strawberries are there? _____

   16 out of every 250 people in the country wear glasses. What is this as a percentage? _____

   A bank paid Anna some interest on the £180 she had in the bank. It paid her £32.
   What is this as a percentage? _____

   A pack of biscuits usually has 20 biscuits. In a new pack, 15% more biscuits are included.
   How many extra biscuits is that? _____

   A drink is made with 18% of the total liquid being blackcurrant juice. If 350 ml of drink is made, how much is blackcurrant juice? _____

   In a phone bill, 17.5% VAT is added to the cost of calls. If the total cost of calls is £58, how much is VAT? _____

2. **Solve these problems, reading the question carefully.**

   45% of the 120 pupils in Class 1W are boys.
   65% of the 80 pupils in Class 2G are boys.
   Which class has more boys? _____

   Megan scored 101 out of 130 in a test.
   Rachel scored 188 out of 220 in a test.
   Which girl had the higher percentage? _____

Percentage increases and decreases

Practice

- When something is made larger, it is **increased**.
  Things can be increased *by a percentage*. Look at these examples:

Salaries are **increased by 25%**.

This packet is **25% larger** than the standard packet.

A 1-month-old baby now weighs **30% more** than at birth.

Notice how the examples show a percentage *and* words like **more**, **larger** or **increased by**.

This black line is **increased by 50%**.

The new line will have an extra 50% added on.

This black line is **increased by 10%**.

The new line will have an extra 10% added on.

This black line is **increased by 100%**.

The new line will have an extra 100% added on.

Notice that a **100% increase** makes the new line **double** the length.

- When something is made smaller it is **decreased**.
  Things can be decreased *by a percentage*. Look at these examples:

Jim now weighs **40% less!**

All prices **reduced by 25%**.

A **12% decrease** in cases of measles last year.

Notice how these examples show a percentage *and* words like **less**, **reduced by** or **decreased by**.

This black line is **decreased by 50%**.

The new line will have 50% taken off.

This black line is **decreased by 10%**.

The new line will have 10% taken off.

This black line is **decreased by 100%**.

The new line will have 100% taken off.

Notice that a **100% decrease** leaves **nothing**.

Clues and tips

Notice that the starting lines are not always the same length.

This means that a **50% increase** for one length might be the *same actual size* as a **100% increase** for another length.

Always look at the *original length* before estimating the size of the increase.

Don't worry about estimating

People sometimes worry that their estimates will be wrong.

Here, estimating just gets you used to giving a rough idea of what percentage is added on.

What next?

If you feel that you understand what a percentage increase or decrease is, you are ready to solve problems with them. Go on to the next page. If not, re-read page 23 and try the examples.

Try it yourself!

1. Estimate these percentage increases.

This black line is **increased** by about ....% of its length.　　**50%**

This black line is **increased** by about ....% of its length.　　_____

This black line is **increased** by about ....% of its length.　　_____

This black line is **increased** by about ....% of its length.　　_____

2. Estimate these percentage decreases.

This black line is **decreased** by about ....% of its length.　　_____

This black line is **decreased** by about ....% of its length.　　_____

This black line is **decreased** by about ....% of its length.　　_____

This black line is **decreased** by about ....% of its length.　　_____

Percentage increases

Practice

- Now that you understand what a **percentage increase** is, you can solve percentage increase problems.
- This is all you have to do:

a) **calculate** the percentage of the amount given

b) **add** it on.

- Here is an example:

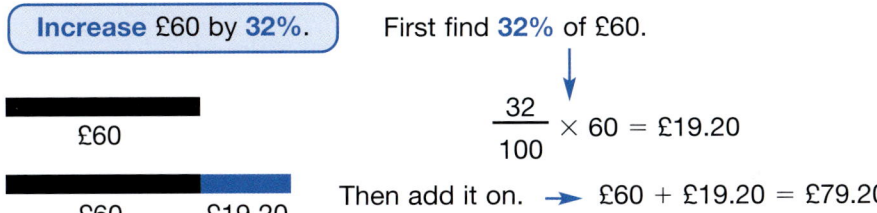

| Increase £60 by **32%**. | First find **32%** of £60. |

$$\frac{32}{100} \times 60 = £19.20$$

Then add it on. → £60 + £19.20 = £79.20

- Here is another example:

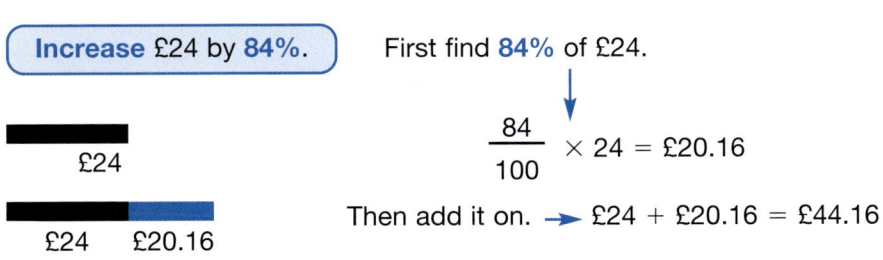

| Increase £24 by **84%**. | First find **84%** of £24. |

$$\frac{84}{100} \times 24 = £20.16$$

Then add it on. → £24 + £20.16 = £44.16

- That is all there is to it, but sometimes the problems are worded in different ways. Try these.

> The number of biscuits in a packet has been **increased by 15%**. There used to be **20** biscuits in a packet. How many are there now?

$$\frac{15}{100} \times 20 = 3$$

20 + 3 = 23

So now there are 23 biscuits altogether.

> There were **4700** people living in a village last year. This year the population has **grown by 36%**. How many people live in the village now?

> In a phone bill, VAT at **17.5% is added** to the cost of calls. The cost of calls is **£48**. How much will the bill be, including VAT?

You can do this already

The first step is easy – you can already do this. See page 13 to remind yourself how.

Use a calculator.

Remember that the percentage sign means 'out of 100' or 'divided by 100', so key in

32 ÷ 100

and then use the × key in place of the word 'of'.

Alternatively, you might prefer to key in the **decimal** 0.32 before multiplying by 60.

The answer will be the same whichever way you do it.

Watch out for words that show an increase, like 'grow', 'more', 'increases', 'added', 'extra', 'larger'.

Try it yourself!

1. Increase each price by the percentage shown.

Increase £80 by **24%** _____   Increase £25 by **64%** _____

Increase £48 by **82%** _____   Increase £93 by **13%** _____

Increase £134 by **47%** _____   Increase £228 by **73%** _____

Remember to check your answers by making a rough approximation.

2. Solve these percentage increase problems.

A car is travelling at a **58 mph**. The driver **increases** the car's speed by **18%**. What is the car's new speed? _____

Last year a man's mass was **58 kg**. This year his mass has **increased** by **12%**. What is the man's mass now? _____

The population of a village has **grown** by **35%** from **1560** people ten years ago. What is the population of the village now? _____

In a phone bill, VAT at **17.5%** is **added** to the total cost of calls. The total cost of calls is **£68**. How much will the bill be including VAT? _____

Remember to check your answers by making a rough approximation.

Percentage decreases

Practice

- Now that you can solve **percentage increase** problems, you will find **percentage decrease** problems just as easy.
- This is all you have to do:

a) **calculate** the percentage of the amount given
b) **subtract** it.

- Here is an example:

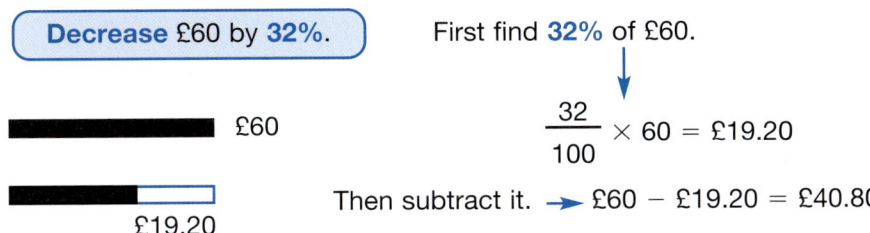

> **Decrease £60 by 32%.**

First find **32%** of £60.

$$\frac{32}{100} \times 60 = £19.20$$

Then subtract it. → £60 − £19.20 = £40.80

- Here is another example:

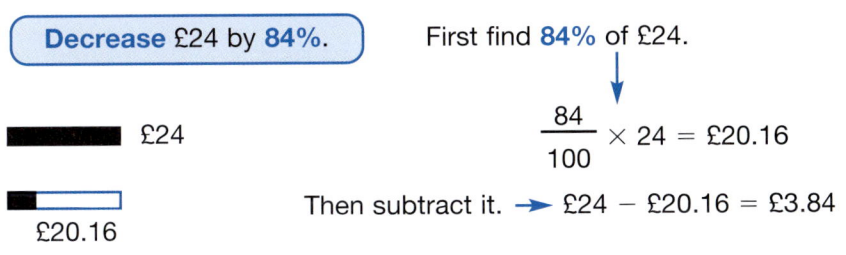

> **Decrease £24 by 84%.**

First find **84%** of £24.

$$\frac{84}{100} \times 24 = £20.16$$

Then subtract it. → £24 − £20.16 = £3.84

- That is all there is to it, but sometimes the problems are worded in different ways. Try these.

> The number of biscuits in a packet has been **decreased by 15%**. There used to be **20** biscuits in a packet. How many are there now?

$$\frac{15}{100} \times 20 = 3$$

20 − 3 = 17
So now there are 17 biscuits altogether.

> There were **4789** people living in a village last year. This year the population has **reduced by 36%**. How many people live in the village now?

> A shop offers a **65% discount** on all ticket prices. A jacket's ticket price is **£28**. How much will the jacket cost in the sale?

Try it yourself!

1. **Decrease** each price by the percentage shown.

Decrease £80 by **24%** _____   Decrease £25 by **64%** _____

Decrease £48 by **82%** _____   Decrease £93 by **13%** _____

Decrease £134 by **47%** _____   Decrease £228 by **73%** _____

Remember to check your answers by making a rough approximation.

2. Solve these **percentage decrease** problems.

A car is travelling at a **58 mph**. The driver **decreases** the car's speed by **18%.** What is the car's new speed? _____

Last year a man's mass was **58 kg**. This year his mass has **fallen** by **12%**. What is the man's mass now? _____

The population of a village has **dropped** by **35%** from **1560** people ten years ago. What is the population of the village now? _____

A person pays **22%** of his earnings in tax. He earns **£28 000** each year. How much money will he have **left** after he has paid tax? _____

Remember to check your answers by making a rough approximation.

Increasing and decreasing more than once

Practice

- **Percentage increases** and **decreases** occur in many situations in **real life**. Look at these examples:

> When a person puts money into a savings account, they receive an extra percentage of that money called **interest**.

> In January, a shop reduces its prices for the sale. Those items not sold by February are reduced by a further percentage.

- In both examples, a percentage increase or decrease occurs *more than once*.

> Emily has £3000 in a bank. She receives 5% interest each year.
> <u>After Year 1:</u>
>   she receives **5%** of **£3000** (= £150), which is added to her money.
> <u>After Year 2:</u>
>   she receives **5%** of **£3150** (= £157.50), which is then added.

Notice that the first increase of 5% (£150) is *not the same amount* as the second increase of 5% (£157.50).

> A dress cost £200 in December. In January it is reduced by 15%. In February it is reduced by a further 15%.
> <u>January:</u>
>   The cost is reduced from **£200** by **15%** (£30 reduction).
> <u>February:</u>
>   The cost is reduced from **£170** by **15%** (£25.50 reduction).

Notice that the first decrease of 15% (£30) is *not the same amount* as the second decrease of 15% (£25.50).

- People often make the mistake of thinking that a percentage increase or decrease will be the same as the one that follows it.
- Is an increase of 10% followed by a further increase of 10% *the same* as an increase of 20%? Look at this example:

> Increase **£300** by **10%**   **10%** of **£300** = £30, £300 + £30 = **£330**

then

> Increase **£330** by **10%**   **10%** of **£330** is £33, £330 + £33 = **£363**

Is this the same as . . . ?

> Increase **£300** by **20%**   **20%** of **£330** is £60, £330 + £60 = **£360**
> The answer is **NO**. They are *not* the same.

Interest
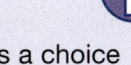

Money kept in a bank or building society account, is usually given interest.

Interest is some extra money that is given, calculated as a percentage of the money that is in the account.

Don't be fooled

Imagine that there was a choice between two bank accounts.

One paid **8%** interest **each year** for **2 years**, and another paid out **16%** interest **after 2 years**. Would both accounts give the same amount of interest after 2 years?

The difference between the two amounts on the left is £3.

More confident with percentages now?

Tick the following topics you feel confident with:

Part 1

Estimating percentages (pages 3–4) ☐

Writing percentages as fractions out of 100 and in their simplest form (pages 5–6) ☐

Writing percentages as fractions and decimals (pages 7–8) ☐

Calculating percentages in your head (pages 9–12) ☐

Calculating percentages with a calculator (pages 13–14) ☐

Part 2

Writing one number as a percentage of another (pages 19–20) ☐

Solving percentage problems (pages 21–22) ☐

Estimating percentage increases and decreases (pages 23–24) ☐

Calculating percentage increases and decreases (pages 25–28) ☐

Increasing and decreasing more than once (pages 29–30) ☐

Read through any pages again to make sure that you understand.

Why not look at other books in this series to help you with areas you still might be unsure about?

Try it yourself!

1. Which is more and by how much?

| £2000 increased by 15%, followed by a further increase of 15% | OR | £2000 increased by 30%? |

15% of £2000 = £300   30% of £2000 = £600
15% of £2300 = £345
Now worth £2645 ←— **More by £45**   Now worth £2600

| £5000 increased by 35%, followed by a further increase of 35% | OR | £5000 increased by 70%? |

| £4000 decreased by 30%, followed by a further decrease of 30% | OR | £4000 decreased by 60%? |

| £9000 decreased by 15%, followed by a further decrease of 15% | OR | £9000 decreased by 30%? |

Answers

ESTIMATING PERCENTAGES (PAGE 4)

These are all estimates. Your answers could be up to 10% different from these answers.

1. About 50%   About 95%   About 10%
   About 75%   About 5%
2. About 75%   About 50%   About 20%
   About 35%   About 80%
3. About 80%   About 90%   About 50%
   About 10%   About 10%
   About 60%   About 70%   About 40%
   About 50%   About 3%

OUT OF 100 (PAGE 5)

$$\frac{50}{100} = \frac{1}{2} \qquad \frac{10}{100} = \frac{1}{10} \qquad \frac{25}{100} = \frac{1}{4}$$

$$\frac{75}{100} = \frac{3}{4} \qquad \frac{20}{100} = \frac{1}{5}$$

OUT OF 100 (PAGE 6)

1. About 80%   About 15%   About 35%
   About 95%

2. $\dfrac{13}{100} \quad \dfrac{27}{100} \quad \dfrac{81}{100} \quad \dfrac{99}{100} \quad \dfrac{39}{100} \quad \dfrac{11}{100} \quad \dfrac{2}{100} \quad \dfrac{47}{100}$

3. $55 \div 100$ $38 \div 100$ $84 \div 100$
   $13 \div 100$ $6 \div 100$ $10 \div 100$

4. $\dfrac{20}{100} = \dfrac{1}{5} \qquad \dfrac{10}{100} = \dfrac{1}{10} \qquad \dfrac{75}{100} = \dfrac{3}{4}$

   $\dfrac{5}{100} = \dfrac{1}{20} \qquad \dfrac{80}{100} = \dfrac{4}{5} \qquad \dfrac{2}{100} = \dfrac{1}{50}$

PERCENTAGES, FRACTIONS AND DECIMALS (PAGE 8)

1. 0.25   0.32   0.67
   0.21   0.86   0.05
   0.03   0.2 (or 0.20)   0.5 (or 0.50)
   0.8 (or 0.80)
2. 0.55   0.35   0.74
   0.18   0.07   0.32
   0.1 (or 0.10)   0.99   1 (or 1.0 or 1.00)
   0.01   0.4 (or 0.40)   0.33

3. 30% $\dfrac{30}{100} = \dfrac{3}{10}$ 0.3   90% $\dfrac{90}{100} = \dfrac{9}{10}$ 0.9

   2% $\dfrac{2}{100} = \dfrac{1}{50}$ 0.02   15% $\dfrac{15}{100} = \dfrac{3}{20}$ 0.15

   8% $\dfrac{8}{100} = \dfrac{2}{25}$ 0.08

CALCULATING PERCENTAGES IN YOUR HEAD (PAGE 10)

1. £300   £60   £340   36 kg   24 kg   420 kg
   £150   £30   £170   18 kg   12 kg   210 kg
   £450   £90   £510   54 kg   36 kg   630 kg
2. £40   £55   £66   35 kg   45 kg   145 kg
   12 ml   105 ml   115 ml   36 m   27 m   92 m
3. £42   £6000   £39

CALCULATING OTHER PERCENTAGES (PAGE 12)

1. £60   £12   £68   7.2 kg   4.8 kg   8.4 kg
   £120   £24   £136   14.4 kg   9.6 kg   16.8 kg
2. £18   £24   £72   28 kg   99 kg   7 kg
   56 ml   48 ml   240 ml   126 m   77 km   55.2 m
3. £48   £3600   117 ounces

CALCULATING PERCENTAGES WITH A CALCULATOR (PAGE 14)

1. £19.20   £30.72   £85.36   29.4 kg
   20.16 kg   16.1 kg   14.79 ml   36.25 ml
   250.1 ml   143.55 m   84.96 m   66.24 m
2. £20.16   £4200   111.8 ounces   36.18 mph
   £12.78   £4.20

WRITING SOMETHING AS A PERCENTAGE (PAGE 20)

1. 80%   85%   92.31%   20%
   72.5%   93.33%   64.29%   61.54%
2. 84%   91.43%   91.25%   82.5%
   87.5%   90%   Richard
3. 40%   60%

PROBLEMS, PROBLEMS (PAGE 22)

1. 35 g   6.4%   17.78%   3 biscuits
   63 ml   £10.15
2. Class 1W has 54 boys, Class 2G has 52 boys
   Megan has 77.69%, Rachel has 85.45%, Rachel has higher percentage.

PERCENTAGE INCREASES AND DECREASES (PAGE 24)

These are estimates. Your answers might be up to 10% different.

1. 50%   100%   25%   200%
2. 25%   68%   90%   100%

Answers

PERCENTAGE INCREASES (PAGE 25)
6392   £56.40

PERCENTAGE INCREASES (PAGE 26)
1. £99.20   £41   £87.36   £105.09
     £196.98   £394.44
2. 68.44 mph 64.96 kg   2106   £79.90

PERCENTAGE DECREASES (PAGE 27)
3065   £9.80

PERCENTAGE DECREASES (PAGE 28)
1. £60.80   £9   £8.64   £80.91
     £71.02   £61.56
2. 47.56 mph 51.04 kg   1014   £21 840

INCREASING AND DECREASING MORE THAN ONCE (PAGE 30)
1. £5000 increased by 35% followed by further increase of 35% = £9112.50. More by £612.50
£5000 increased by 70% = £8500

£4000 decreased by 30% followed by further decrease of 30% = £1960. More by £360
£4000 decreased by 60% = £1600

£9000 decreased by 15% followed by further decrease of 15% = £6502.50. More by £202.50
£9000 decreased by 30% = £6300